First World War
and Army of Occupation
War Diary
France, Belgium and Germany

19 DIVISION
Divisional Troops
Royal Army Medical Corps
Divisional Field Ambulance Workshop Unit
16 July 1915 - 6 April 1916

WO95/2073/2

The Naval & Military Press Ltd
www.nmarchive.com
Published in association with The National Archives

Published by

The Naval & Military Press Ltd

Unit 10 Ridgewood Industrial Park,

Uckfield, East Sussex,

TN22 5QE England

Tel: +44 (0) 1825 749494

www.naval-military-press.com

www.nmarchive.com

This diary has been reprinted in facsimile from the original. Any imperfections are inevitably reproduced and the quality may fall short of modern type and cartographic standards.

© **Crown Copyright**
Images reproduced by permission of The National Archives, London, England, 2015.

Contents

Document type	Place/Title	Date From	Date To
Heading	WO95/2073/2 19 Divn Divisional Field Amb Work Shop		
Heading	19th Fd Amb. Workshop Unit. Jly 1915-Apr 1916		
Heading	19th Division 19th F.A.W.U. Vol I July To Oct 15		
War Diary	Avonmouth	16/07/1915	17/07/1915
War Diary	Southampton	17/07/1915	17/07/1915
War Diary	Rouen	18/07/1915	22/07/1915
War Diary	Neufchatel	23/07/1915	23/07/1915
War Diary	St. Omer	24/07/1915	25/07/1915
War Diary	Guarbecque	26/07/1915	28/07/1915
War Diary	St Hilaire	29/07/1915	30/07/1915
War Diary	Corbeille	31/07/1915	09/08/1915
War Diary	Calonne	10/08/1915	27/08/1915
War Diary	Eglise	28/08/1915	12/09/1915
War Diary	Les Lobes	13/09/1915	31/10/1915
Heading	19th Division Nov 15		
War Diary	Les Lobes	01/11/1915	23/11/1915
War Diary	Les Lobes Merville	24/11/1915	24/11/1915
War Diary	Merville	25/11/1915	25/11/1915
War Diary	Merville St Venant	26/11/1915	26/11/1915
War Diary	St Venant	27/11/1915	30/11/1915
Heading	19th Division 19th F.A.W.U. Vol. 3.		
War Diary	St Venant	01/12/1915	04/12/1915
War Diary	St Venant Locon	05/12/1915	05/12/1915
War Diary	Locon	06/12/1915	10/12/1915
War Diary	Locon Lestrem	11/12/1915	11/12/1915
War Diary	Lestrem	12/12/1915	31/12/1915
Heading	19th F.A.W.U. Vol 4 Jan 1916		
War Diary	Lestrem	01/01/1916	24/01/1916
War Diary	Robecque	25/01/1916	31/01/1916
Heading	19th Y.A.W.U. Feb 1916		
Heading	19th Y.A.W.U. Vol 5		
War Diary	Robecque	01/02/1916	16/02/1916
War Diary	Merville	18/02/1916	29/02/1916
Heading	War Diaries of 19th Divisional Field Ambulance Workshop Unit-A.S.C., for the Months of March And April 1916		
Heading	19th Div F.A.W.U Vol 6		
Miscellaneous	Per Registered Post To D.A.O. a. H. O 3rd Echelon	31/03/1916	31/03/1916
War Diary	Merville	01/03/1916	31/03/1916
Heading	19th F.A.W.U. Vol 6 Appendix		
War Diary	Merville	01/04/1916	06/04/1916

WO95 2073/2

19 DIVN
DIVISIONAL FIELD AMB. WORKSHOP UNIT
1915 JULY - 1916 APRIL

19TH DIVISION

19TH FD AMB. WORKSHOP UNIT.

JLY 1915-APR 1916

121/7593

19th Division

July – Oct. 1915

19th F.A.X.U.
Vol I
July to Oct. 15

Apl. '16

Army Form C. 2118.

WAR DIARY
or
INTELLIGENCE SUMMARY.
(Erase heading not required.)

Instructions regarding War Diaries and Intelligence Summaries are contained in F. S. Regs., Part II. and the Staff Manual respectively. Title pages will be prepared in manuscript.

Place	Date	Hour	Summary of Events and Information	Remarks and references to Appendices
AVONMOUTH	16/4/15	6.0 p.m.	Left MARLBOROUGH at 2.a.m.; arrived AVONMOUTH 9.15 a.m.; embarked cars; 15 "Sunbeams" and 4 "Fords" on "S.S. TREVAYLOR"; Workshop, Stores Van and "Daimler" lorry on "S.S. MONTA"; billeted at Rest Camp.	DSC
SOUTHAMPTON	17/4/15	6.0 p.m.	Left AVONMOUTH by G.W.R at 10 a.m.; arrived SOUTHAMPTON 2.p.m.; men embarked 5.30p.m; Sailed 7.30 p.m on "S.S. ST PETERSBURG".	DSC
ROUEN	18/4/15	6.0 p.m.	Arrived ROUEN at 10.a.m. after uneventful voyage; marched to Rest Camp; Cpl. Parker in charge of workshop. Stores Van & "Daimler" arrived at LE HAVRE; medical officer's inspection.	DSC
ROUEN	19/4/15	6.0 p.m.	Medical officer inoculated Company at Station Hospital; Cpl. Parker dis-embarked at LE HAVRE with workshop and stores.	DSC
ROUEN	20/4/15	6.0 p.m.	Cpl. Parker followed 20th Div. Supply Column with workshop and stores; arriving in ROUEN at 2.30 p.m.; "Daimler" lorry arrived ROUEN by steamer - disembarked and parked; Reveille 5.30a.m.; Cars disembarked and driven to lines; Staff Sergt Cannion was driving No. 8 "Sunbeam" Ambulance, met with accident in Rue Belge. ROUEN; car badly damaged; S.S. Cannion taken in charge by M.P. for being drunk whilst on duty in charge of car; accident reported to O.C. by Sergt Crawford who was with prisoner.	DSC

1577 Wt. W10731/1773 500,000 7/15 D.D.&L. A.D.S.S./Forms/C. 2118.

WAR DIARY
or
INTELLIGENCE SUMMARY.
(Erase heading not required.)

Army Form C. 2118.

Instructions regarding War Diaries and Intelligence Summaries are contained in F. S. Regs. Part II. and the Staff Manual respectively. Title pages will be prepared in manuscript.

Place	Date	Hour	Summary of Events and Information	Remarks and references to Appendices
ROUEN	21/4/15	6.0 p.m.	The remainder of Company inoculated. Usual routine.	D.B.
ROUEN	22/4/15	6.0 p.m.	General clean up; ready to move; 19th Supply and Ammunition Columns left at 3 o'clock; S.S. Platt H - M/18538 seconded to this Unit from 3rd Echelon, ROUEN.	D.B.
NEUFCHÂTEL	23/4/15	8.0 p.m.	Parade 6.30 a.m.; Ptes Sims, Read, Moore, Butler, Case and Smart absent from parade; punishment awarded — extra drills; Left ROUEN 3 p.m.; arrived NEUFCHÂTEL 6.15 p.m.; Serge. Crawford, having been remanded for evidence in connection with the C.M. of S.S. Cunnison, was left at ROUEN, the O.C., M.T. Depôt, ROUEN, being asked to arrange for him to follow Unit at the conclusion of Court Martial.	D.B.
ST. OMER	24/4/15	9.0 p.m.	Left NEUFCHÂTEL at 8.30 a.m.; proceeded to ABEVILLE where a "Sunbeam" car in place of the one smashed by S.S. Cunnison was received; then proceeded to ST. OMER, arriving there at 7.0 p.m.; Pte. Marshall f.-M/2-022064 at ABEVILLE with new car.	D.B.
ST. OMER	25/4/15	6.0 p.m.	Cars cleaned up and adjustments made; lettering on sides of "Sunbeams" painted out; N.C.O's + men paid.	D.B.

Army Form C. 2118.

WAR DIARY
or
INTELLIGENCE SUMMARY.
(Erase heading not required.)

Instructions regarding War Diaries and Intelligence Summaries are contained in F. S. Regs., Part II. and the Staff Manual respectively. Title pages will be prepared in manuscript.

Place	Date	Hour	Summary of Events and Information	Remarks and references to Appendices
GUARBECQUE	26/7/15	6.0 p.m.	Left St. OMER at 10.30 a.m. No 1. Section (57th Field Ambulance) proceeded to AIRE. - 17min 7cars " 2 " (58th " " ") " " ST. HILAIRE - 17min 7cars " 3 " (59th " " ") " " GUARBECQUE - 17min 7cars Workshop, Store Van, Daimler, Officer's car and 20 men also " Sergt. Crawford still absent.	W.B.
GUASBECQUE	27/7/15	6.0 p.m.	Men and Ambulances of Sections 1, 2 & 3 officially handed over to R.A.M.C. with Pay Books and A.F. B.122; Reveille 6 o'clock; Parade 9.0 a.m. for drivers of vehicles only.	W.B.
GUASBECQUE	28/7/15	6.0 p.m.	Reveille 6.0 a.m.; Parade 9.a.m.; Usual routine.	W.B.
ST. HILAIRE	29/7/15	6.0 p.m.	Workshop, Stores Van and "Daimler" lorry left GUASBECQUE at 9.0 a.m. and proceeded to ST. HILAIRE where we joined the 58th F.A. Pte Snailum, Lowe and Locke attached to workshop staff as clerk, Officer's Driver, and Officer's servant respectively.	W.B.
ST. HILAIRE	30/7/15	6.0 p.m.	Remained at ST. HILAIRE. Ambulances inspected by Colonel at 2 p.m. L.C. Snailum R.J - MA - 080923 to be Acting Corpl; assistant to Q.M.S. with Pay.	W.B.
CORBEILLE	31/7/15	6.0 p.m.	Workshop, Stores Van and Daimler, & 58th F.A. Left ST. HILAIRE at 12.30 and proceeded to CORBEILLE arriving at 6.0 p.m. in an orchard.	W.B.

WAR DIARY
or
INTELLIGENCE SUMMARY.
(Erase heading not required.)

Army Form C. 2118.

Instructions regarding War Diaries and Intelligence Summaries are contained in F.S. Regs, Part II. and the Staff Manual respectively. Title pages will be prepared in manuscript.

Place	Date	Hour	Summary of Events and Information	Remarks and references to Appendices
CORBEILLE	1/8/15	6.0 pm	"Ladies of Buckinghamshire" car brought in for repairs, springs buckled. Usual routine.	B.E.
CORBEILLE	2/8/15	6.0 pm	Pte SHAW - M/2/052030 cautioned for taking and using iron from stores without permission. D.A.D.M.S. asked to replace BUCKINGHAMSHIRE car with more suitable Ambulance. Heavy rain and thunderstorm.	B.E.
CORBEILLE	3/8/15	6.0 pm	100 galls petrol fetched from Railhead. "FORD" Ambulance "A.7" brought in for repair. ACTING CORPL. STADDEN. J.T. M/2/049845 cautioned for leaving quarters without permission. Rained heavily.	B.E.
CORBEILLE	4/8/15	6.0 pm	ACT. SERGT. CRAWFORD. A.R. M/2/078110 reported himself for duty in the forenoon, upon conclusion of the CM of S.S. CUNNION. 50 empty petrol tins returned to Railhead. Repairs to "FORD" Ambulance "A.7" completed. Stowery.	B.E.
CORBEILLE	5/8/15	6.0 pm	ACT: CPL: STADDEN. J.T. and PTE SHAW RD. reported sick. Packed up ready to move at any moment. Fine.	B.E.
CORBEILLE	6/8/15	6.0 pm	ACT: CPL: STADDEN. J.T. again reported sick. "SUNBEAM" Ambulance "C.15" came in for repairs with bent front axle and damaged front tyre. New tyre supplied and car sent out same night repaired. Motor cycle attached to 5yd F.A. brought in	B.E.

WAR DIARY
or
INTELLIGENCE SUMMARY.
(Erase heading not required.)

Army Form C. 2118.

Place	Date	Hour	Summary of Events and Information	Remarks and references to Appendices
			(Continued)	
CORBEILLE	6/8/15	6.0 p.m	- for alterations to magneto chain. Dull, some rain.	DRB
CORBEILLE	7/8/15	"	Act: Corpl: STADDEN taken to Hospital at ST. VENANT suffering from acute tonsilitis. BUCKINGHAMSHIRE car again came in. Dull.	DRB
CORBEILLE	8/8/15	"	100 galls. Petrol fetched from Railhead. Usual Routine.	DRB
CORBEILLE	9/8/15	"	50 galls Petrol to 57th F.A; Staff-Sergt PLATT.H.M/18538 on leave for one week. Dull, some rain.	DRB
CALLONNE	10/8/15	"	Left CORBEILLE at 8.30 a.m - arrived CALLONNE 9.30 a.m. Took BUCKINGHAMSHIRE Car with us. 100 gallons petrol fetched. Not-close.	DRB
CALLONNE	11/8/15	"	50 galls petrol to 59th F.A; "men fired"; Actg: Corpl. STADDEN J.T., still in Hospital. Hot-close.	DRB
CALLONNE	12/8/15	"	50 galls petrol to 57th F.A; repairs (alterations) to BUCKINGHAMSHIRE Car completed. Rainy. Pte's BADDOCK, SHAW, & BUTLER nail allotments; notification sent to Regt: Paymaster, Woolwich.	DRB
CALLONNE	13/8/15	"	100 Galls. Petrol fetched from Railhead. Usual routine. Rainy.	DRB

WAR DIARY
or
INTELLIGENCE SUMMARY.
(Erase heading not required.)

Army Form C. 2118.

Instructions regarding War Diaries and Intelligence Summaries are contained in F. S. Regs., Part II. and the Staff Manual respectively. Title pages will be prepared in manuscript.

Place	Date	Hour	Summary of Events and Information	Remarks and references to Appendices
CALONNE	14/8/15	6 p.m.	Usual Routine. Weekly returns despatched.	B.
CALONNE	15/8/15	6 p.m.	100 gallons of petrol fetched from Railhead. Usual Routine. Rainy.	B.
CALONNE	16/8/15	6 p.m.	50 gallons of petrol to 57th F.A and 59th F.A. Return of all cars giving particulars of chassis, engine no. &c., sent to D.D. of S.+T. Thunderstorm and heavy rain.	B.
CALONNE	17/8/15	6 p.m.	100 gallons of petrol fetched from Railhead. M.S.S. PLATT - M/18538 - returned from leave of absence at 12.30 p.m. Thunderstorm - heavy rain.	B.
CALONNE	18/8/15	6 p.m.	M²/079845 - CPL. STADDEN. J.T. returned from hospital, reported at 12.0. o'clock. Men paid. Arrangements made for C.Q.M. SGT. TAYLOR to visit the three F.A's, ascertain their requirements and report to O.C. Rained very heavily during the morning.	B.
CALONNE	19/8/15	6 p.m.	Men cautioned by O.C. on parade with regard to the waste of rations and use of latrines. Stock of stokes taken. 100 gallons of petrol fetched from Railhead. "SUNBEAM" ambulance "B12" in for repairs. Fine	B.

WAR DIARY
or
INTELLIGENCE SUMMARY.
(Erase heading not required.)

Army Form C. 2118.

Place	Date	Hour	Summary of Events and Information	Remarks and references to Appendices
CALONNE	20/8/15	6.0 p.m.	M². 052965 - Act. Cpl. Jones warned by O.C. for refusal to obey orders of C.Q.M Sgt. Taylor. Lieut. Bradley visited D.A.D.M.S. St. OMER, who approved of the alterations effected to the BUCKINGHAMSHIRE ambulance. Fine.	WB
CALONNE	21/8/15	6.0 p.m.	M². 079842. Pte. CHARLTON W.G. reports sick and is taken to No. 7. Casualty Clearing Hospital, MERVILLE. LIEUT. BRADLEY personally delivered weekly returns to D.D. of S.T. Active Service log Books compiled and issued to 59th F.A. Officer's car repainted. 100 gallons of petrol fetched from Railhead. Several heavy storms during the day.	WB
CALONNE	22/8/15	6.0 p.m.	Painting of Officer's car completed. Active Service log Books issued to 57th & 59th F.A's. Roll to be called nightly at 8.30 posted in Orders. Fine.	WB
CALONNE	23/8/15	6.0 p.m.	M². 052965 - Act. Cpl. JONES reports sick. M². 079214 Pte. PROBYN - (O.C. 58th Divn. F.A.) to 14 days CB each Pte STREET to be fined 21 days pay and Pte BALDOCK 14 days pay for (1) Being drunk on active service and (2) Being absent off Pass from 8.15 p.m. on 21/8/15 to 9.20 p.m. on 21/8/15 (1 hr). 100 gallons of petrol fetched from Railhead. Fine.	WB

WAR DIARY
or
INTELLIGENCE SUMMARY.
(Erase heading not required.)

Army Form C. 2118.

Place	Date	Hour	Summary of Events and Information	Remarks and references to Appendices
CALONNE	24/8/15	6.0 pm	1 Drum and 30-2 lb. tins of Carbide fetched from Railhead. The 58th F.A. held very successful swimming sports in the afternoon and provided a Concert in the evening. Fine.	D.S.B.
CALONNE	25/8/15	6.0 pm	46 gallons of Petrol from Railhead. Men paid at 2.0 pm. Usual Routine. Fine.	D.S.B.
CALONNE	26/8/15	6.0 pm	Usual Routine. Fine.	D.S.B.
CALONNE	27/8/15	6.0 pm	50 gallons of Petrol to 59th F.A. Men attended washing baths in Merville in the afternoon. Weather sultry.	D.S.B.
ÉGLISE	28/8/15	6.0 pm	Reveillé 5 a.m. Packed and ready to start by 9.30 a.m. Left CALONNE 3 pm. arrived ÉGLISE 3.30 pm. Unit stationed by itself in orchard. Weekly returns despatched.	D.S.B.
ÉGLISE	29/8/15	6.0 pm	100 gallons petrol fetched from Railhead, 50 gallons each to 58th & 59th. M.T. 079842. Pte CHARLTON. W.G. returned from hospital, reporting at 4.0 pm. Overcast, rained heavily during evening and night.	D.S.B.

WAR DIARY
or
INTELLIGENCE SUMMARY.

Army Form 2118.

Place	Date	Hour	Summary of Events and Information	Remarks and references to Appendices
ÉGLISE	30/8/15	6.0 pm	M² 052965. ACT. CPL JONES. R.M. charged with stealing cigarettes from the baths at MERVILLE on the 27th AUGUST and sentenced by Lt. Col. PROBYN OC. 58th Divn. F.A. to be deprived of his acting rank, fined 7 days pay and awarded 7 days C.B. "SUNBEAM" ambulance "A5" brought in for repairs to back spring. Showery.	1>B
ÉGLISE	31/8/15	6.0 pm	Monthly returns despatched. M² 098153 - PTE. HANDSCOMBE W.J.P. promoted to acting Lance Corporal. 50 gallons of petrol fetched from Railhead. Dull, but no rain.	1>B

WAR DIARY
or
INTELLIGENCE SUMMARY.
(Erase heading not required.)

Army Form C. 2118.

Place	Date	Hour	Summary of Events and Information	Remarks and references to Appendices
ÉGLISE	1/9/15	6.0.p.m.	M.T. O5D4442. Pte STANLEY. M.T. sentenced to 14 days CB by LIEUT. BRADLEY for conduct to the prejudice of good order and military discipline. Guard re-arranged so that Corp. in charge is on duty from 6 p.m. to 10 p.m., the other two shifts being from 10 p.m. to 2 a.m. and from 2 a.m. to 6 a.m. Routine orders re passes when riding on lorry or car received from D.A.Q.M.G. Some rain during the evening	D.W.B.
ÉGLISE	2/9/15	6 p.m.	Routine Orders read by LIEUT. BRADLEY on parade. Ran through stock of stationery; 100 galls of petrol fetched from Railhead. Raining intermittently all day.	D.W.B
ÉGLISE	3/9/15	6 p.m.	Men shift sleeping quarters from field to barn adjacent to farm house, on account of the inclement weather. Slight accident to LIEUT. BRADLEY due to backfire when starting car; 126 gallons of petrol fetched from Railhead. Raining steadily all day.	D.W.B
ÉGLISE	4/9/15	6 p.m.	Weekly returns compiled and despatched. DD of S.&T. returns taken by LIEUT. BRADLEY. Men given half holiday. Raining all day without inter-mission.	D.W.B

Army Form C. 2118.

WAR DIARY
or
INTELLIGENCE SUMMARY.
(Erase heading not required.)

Instructions regarding War Diaries and Intelligence Summaries are contained in F. S. Regs., Part II. and the Staff Manual respectively. Title pages will be prepared in manuscript.

Place	Date	Hour	Summary of Events and Information	Remarks and references to Appendices
EGLISE	5/9/15	6.0pm	M² 079214 Pte Street S transferred on authority of the DADT to the LAHORE DIVISIONAL SUPPLY column with AFB 122. Receipt obtained. Usual routine; raining in the morning.	
EGLISE	6/9/15	6.0pm	Extra stores ordered as per revised G.1098; 100 gallons of petrol fetched from Railhead. Usual routine. Fine, warm.	
EGLISE	7/9/15	6.0pm	Usual routine. Fine, warm.	
EGLISE	8/9/15	6.0pm	Men paid at 2 p.m; Kit inspection at 2.15 p.m. and deficiencies made good. Fine, warm.	
EGLISE	9/9/15	6.0pm	Surplus clothing stores handed over to LIEUT Q. MASTER, 58 FIELD AMBULANCE. Men again warned in daily orders re the necessity of boiling water used for drinking purposes. 100 gallons of petrol from Railhead. Fine, warm.	
EGLISE	10/9/15	6.0pm	Usual routine. Fine, warm.	
EGLISE	11/9/15	6.0pm	96 gallons of petrol from Railhead. Weekly returns despatched. Returns for D.D. of S. taken by LIEUT. BRADLEY. Usual Routine. Fine, warm.	
EGLISE	12/9/15	6.0pm	Usual routine. Fine warm.	

T2134. Wt. W708—776. 500000. 4/15. Sir J. C. & E.

WAR DIARY
or
INTELLIGENCE SUMMARY.
(Erase heading not required.)

Army Form C. 2118.

Place	Date	Hour	Summary of Events and Information	Remarks and references to Appendices
LES LOBES	13/9/15	6.0 pm	Packed up and left ÉGLISE on very short notice at 10.a.m; arrived LES LOBES at 10.30 a.m. Workshop fixed up in courtyard of French farmhouse. Men sleeping in loft. Fine, warm. 100 gallons petrol from Railhead.	
LES LOBES	14/9/15	6.0 pm	General clean up of vehicles and yard. O.C. called away at 10 p.m. to attend to pump at the troops' baths at LOCON. Some friction between the C.Q.M.S. and S.Sgt. Rain during the morning. Dull.	
LES LOBES	15/9/15	6.0 pm	Men cautioned on parade with regard to the lack of respect shewn to the O.C. when addressed by him. Posted in orders that the S.Sgt. controls routine work, subject to the subsequent supervision by the C.Q.M.Sgt. Weather dull.	
LES LOBES	16/9/15	6.0 pm	Usual routine. 100 galls. petrol from Railhead. Dull - clear.	
LES LOBES	17/9/15	6.0 pm	Two Sunbeam Ambulance, 1 Ford, - 2 motor cycles in for repairs. Arrangement made with O.C. 5 Fld. F.A. to repaint Ambulances systematically. Workshop running till 8.0 pm. Fine.	
LES LOBES	18/9/15	6.0 pm	Returns compiled. O.C. personally handed in returns to D.D of S+T. Certain Routine Orders posted up for the information of N.C.O's and men. Information received from DD of S+T, that 5 cars from Divisional Train, 1 car and	

WAR DIARY
or
INTELLIGENCE SUMMARY.

(Erase heading not required.)

Army Form C. 2118.

Instructions regarding War Diaries and Intelligence Summaries are contained in F. S. Regs, Part II. and the Staff Manual respectively. Title pages will be prepared in manuscript.

Place	Date	Hour	Summary of Events and Information	Remarks and references to Appendices
LES LOBES	18/9/15	(continued)	One lorry from Divisional Signals, and one lorry from Divisional Sanitary Section, attached to this Unit for minor repairs. O.C. visited and made necessary arrangement re supplies etc. 76 gallons of petrol from Railhead. Fine, warm.	
LES LOBES	19/9/15	6.0pm	N° 079842. Pte CHARLTON W.G. to hospital. Four Douglas motor cycles received, frame nos. 18292, 17937, 18228, 20883. Fine, warm.	
LES LOBES	20/9/15	6.0pm	Morning parade altered from 8.0 a.m. to 7.30 a.m. 20 galls of petrol needed daily for DIVISIONAL TRAIN Cars. Supply of petrol increased from 296 to 476 gallons per week. Question raised as to supplies, repairs etc, for DIVISIONAL TRAIN and DIVISIONAL SIGNALS.— both asked to get supplies etc. through the same channels as before, pending definite arrangement. Extra tyres and tubes ordered. The OsC de three FA's asked to arrange for steps at back of Ambulances always to be kept up. Douglas cycles tested by O.C. and found to be satisfactory. 150 gallons of petrol from Railhead.	

WAR DIARY
or
INTELLIGENCE SUMMARY.
(Erase heading not required.)

Army Form C. 118.

Place	Date	Hour	Summary of Events and Information	Remarks and references to Appendices
LES LOBES	21/9/15	6.0 p.m.	Petrol supply reduced to 326 gallons per week in view of above. M² 079842 Pte CHARLTON W.G. returned from Hospital. Report sent by O.C. to A.D.M.S re use of Ambulances for hauling Stores &c. Weather – fine.	A.3
LES LOBES	22/9/15	6.0 p.m.	Lorry attached to SANITARY SECTION sent to ISBERGUES to be re-tyred. Men paid at 2.p.m. Allotment of 6476 – C.Q.M.S. Taylor D.G. raised from 4/- to 5/- per day. A.F. O.1796 sent to Woolwich Paymaster. Fine.	A.3
LES LOBES	23/9/15	6.0 p.m.	N.C.O's and men attended baths at LOCON at 10.30 a.m. 150 galls of petrol from Railhead. Very heavy storm in the evening.	A.3
LES LOBES	24/9/15	6.0 p.m.	M² 052030 Pte SHAW R.D. cautioned by O.C. for alleged neglect of duty whilst on guard. M² 079842 Pte CHARLTON W.G. lodged complaint re work entailed at meal times through waiting on Sergts. D.D. of S.T asked whether the services of M18538 S.Sgt PLATT H. might be better employed elsewhere. O.C. called out at 10.p.m. to attend to breakdown of the Lorry attached to SANITARY SECTION, arrived back in Workshops at 5.0 a.m on 25/9/15. Incessant rain. close.	A.3

WAR DIARY
or
INTELLIGENCE SUMMARY.
(Erase heading not required.)

Army Form C. 2118.

Place	Date	Hour	Summary of Events and Information	Remarks and references to Appendices
LES LOBES	25/9/15	6.0 p.m.	Weekly returns compiled. Returns for D.D. of S.&T. personally taken by O.C. 26 galls petrol from Railhead. Two DOUGLAS motor cycles frame nos. 19539 and 17829 from Railhead. Rained steadily all day.	1363
LES LOBES	26/9/15	6.0 p.m.	150 galls of petrol from Railhead. Workshop staff given half holiday. Voluntary Church parade at 6.0 p.m. No rain but very dull.	1363
LES LOBES	27/9/15	6.0 p.m.	150 galls of petrol from Railhead. Weekly supply again increased to 426 galls. A.D.M.S. queried when miniature lamps on steering arms of Ambulances would be ready. Rained heavily during afternoon and evening.	1363
LES LOBES	28/9/15	6.0 p.m.	50 galls of petrol from Railhead. Magnetos despatched to ADVANCED M.T. DEPOT for re-winding. O.C. F.A.s asked to issue instructions to their motor drivers always to bring their Repair Service Log Books with them when their cars come to the Workshop for repair. Incessant rain.	1363 1365
LES LOBES	29/9/15	6.0 p.m.	150 Galls of petrol from Railhead. Usual routine. Raining all day.	1363
LES LOBES	30/9/15	6.0 p.m.	M⁰ 105913 Pte FOGGIN R.L. received from DIVISIONAL SUPPLY COLUMN and sent to 59th F.A. Monthly returns compiled. 50 gallon petrol from Railhead. Raining during afternoon and evening.	1363

WAR DIARY
or
INTELLIGENCE SUMMARY.

(Erase heading not required.)

Army Form C. 2118.

Place	Date	Hour	Summary of Events and Information	Remarks and references to Appendices
LES LOBES	1/10/15	6.0 pm	100 gallons of petrol from Railhead. Usual routine, dull.	(B)
LES LOBES	2/10/15	6.0 pm	First frost, much colder. Orders received to move; everything packed in readiness, when order was rescinded. G.R.U's 1168 - 1169 read out on parade for the first time. 100 gallons of petrol from Railhead. Men paid at 5 pm.	(B)
LES LOBES	3/10/15	6.0 pm	Stores unpacked. G.R.U's 1168 + 1169 read out on parade for the second time. Question raised as to whether the present system of the Guard, is suitable during the winter. M. 078398 Pte LOCKE W.C. attended hospital with badly cut hand – light duties. Fine, but cold.	(B)
LES LOBES	4/10/15	6.0 pm	Posted in orders that spells of Guard in future shall be as follows:- 1st Spell (Corpl of the Guard), 6 pm –10.30 pm; 2nd Spell 10.30 pm to 1 am; 3rd Spell 1 am to 3.30 am; 4th Spell 3.30 am to 6 am. Car received from DIVISIONAL TRAIN at 5 pm with broken back spring. Men again warned of the necessity of being present at Roll Call at 8.30 pm. Raining all the morning and afternoon	(B)

WAR DIARY
or
INTELLIGENCE SUMMARY.
(Erase heading not required.)

Army Form C. 2118.

Place	Date	Hour	Summary of Events and Information	Remarks and references to Appendices
LES LOBES	5/10/15	6.0 pm	100 Galls Petrol; 60 lbs Carbide from Railhead. Car from DIVISIONAL TRAIN sent out, duty repaired at 8.45 p.m.; Workshops running until 8.45 p.m. Raining intermittently all day.	1&3
LES LOBES	6/10/15	6.0 pm	Men paid at 6.30 p.m. Usual routine. Dull but no rain.	1&3
LES LOBES	7/10/15	6.0 pm	SUNBEAM Ambulance A3 towed into Workshops from 57ᵗʰ FIELD AMBULANCE for overhaul. O.C visited ADVANCED M.T. DEPOT, re stores on order. 150 gallons petrol from Railhead. Fine	1&3
LES LOBES	8/10/15	6.0 pm	Pte ANULTY H - 45447 received for test as fitter & turner. Vulcanizer despatched to ADVANCED M.T. DEPOT. Enquiry received from DD of S.T. re establishment of motor cycles. Workshops running until 9 p.m. Dull, but no rain.	1&3
LES LOBES	9/10/15	6.0 pm	M² 079842 - Pte CHARLTON W.G. reports sick; Pte ANULTY returned - test satisfactory. Thresh disinfector towed from Distillery at FOSSE to Brewery at VIELLE CHAPELLE. Workshops running until 1.30 a.m on 10/10/15. Dull.	1&3

WAR DIARY
or
INTELLIGENCE SUMMARY.
(Erase heading not required.)

Army Form 2118.

Instructions regarding War Diaries and Intelligence Summaries are contained in F. S. Regs., Part II. and the Staff Manual respectively. Title pages will be prepared in manuscript.

Place	Date	Hour	Summary of Events and Information	Remarks and references to Appendices
LES LOBES	10/10/15	6.0.p.m.	100 Galls Petrol from Railhead. M28338 Sgt. Seymour A.W. arrived from 55th Co. A.S.C. St Omer at 4pm. with temporary A.F.B 122. Manual Routine. Fine.	A.S.B.
LES LOBES	11/10/15	6.0.p.m.	100 Gall Petrol from Railhead. 2nd Lt. BRADLEY applies to O.C. 58th FIELD AMBULANCE for 7 days leave from 14/10/15. Rain during afternoon and evening.	A.S.B.
LES LOBES	12/10/15	6.0.p.m.	SUNBEAM from DIVISIONAL TRAIN brought to WORKSHOPS for repairs after slight accident. WORKSHOP running until 8.30.p.m. Fine, bright.	A.S.B.
LES LOBES	13/10/15	6.0.p.m.	100 Galls Petrol from Railhead. M⁄M No.078398 Pte. LOCKE W.C. ceases to attend hospital. Men paid at 6.30.p.m. SUNBEAM from DIVISIONAL TRAIN sent out repaired. WORKSHOP running until 8.0.p.m. Fine, crisp.	A.S.B.
LES LOBES	14/10/15	6.0.p.m.	Arrangements made with A.D.M.S. to make 300 strap for trench stretchers material ordered from D.A.D.O.S. 2nd Lt. GRANT-DALTON detailed by O.C. DIVL SUPPY COLUMN to superintend during Lt. BRADLEY's absence. Miniature headlights on steering arms of Ambulances completed. Fine.	A.S.B.

Army Form C. 2118.

WAR DIARY
or
INTELLIGENCE SUMMARY.
(Erase heading not required.)

Instructions regarding War Diaries and Intelligence Summaries are contained in F. S. Regs., Part II. and the Staff Manual respectively. Title pages will be prepared in manuscript.

Place	Date	Hour	Summary of Events and Information	Remarks and references to Appendices
LES LOBES	15/10/15	6.0 pm	O.C. commenced seven days leave of absence from midnight 15.10.15. Usual Routine. Dull, misty.	
LES LOBES	16/10/15	6.0 pm	2nd Lt. GRANT DALTON of 19th DIVNL. SUPPLY COLUMN superintends work of Unit whilst O.C. is away. Weekly returns compiled and despatched. Dull, misty.	
LES LOBES	17/10/15	6.0 pm	150 Gallons of Petrol from Railhead. Instructions received from CAPT. NILSON of 19th DIVNL. SUPPLY COLUMN to send M/8538 - M.S.S PLATT.H. to 358 Coy. A.S.C. ST. OMER. N°. 079842 Pte CHARLTON W.G to hospital at 58th FIELD AMBULANCE. Fine.	
LES LOBES	18/10/15	6.0 pm	M/8538 - M.S.S PLATT. H. transferred to 358 Coy. A.S.C. ST. OMER - temporary A.F.B/122 being sent with him. Usual Routine. Fine, windy.	
LES LOBES	19/10/15	6.0 pm	150 Gallons of Petrol from Railhead. Usual routine. Fine, crisp.	
LES LOBES	20/10/15	6.0 pm	Usual routine. Fine, bright. 57th FIELD AMBULANCE moved to LOCON. 58th " " " BOIS DE PACAUT 59th " " " " 4th " " " MESPLEAUX.	
LES LOBES	21/10/15	6.0 pm	Usual routine. Rained during the evening.	

WAR DIARY
or
INTELLIGENCE SUMMARY.
(Erase heading not required.)

Army Form C. 2118.

Place	Date	Hour	Summary of Events and Information	Remarks and references to Appendices
LES LOBES	22/10/15	6.0pm	100 gallons of petrol from Railhead; O.C. returns from leave of absence at midnight. Usual routine. Fine crisp.	ADSS
LES LOBES	23/10/15	6.0pm	4 SUNBEAM Ambulance, 1 lorry and one motor cycle in for repairs; Returns compiled and despatched. Report re the attaching of the vehicles of DIVISIONAL TRAIN, SANITARY SECTION and SIGNALS sent to for minor repairs sent to A.D.M.S. Usual Routine. Fine.	ADSS
LES LOBES	24/10/15	6.0pm	M₂.079842 Pte CHARLTON N.G. returned from hospital; C.R.O. re special winter clothing received — necessary equipment ordered from D.A.D.O.S. NORTH LANCS again occupy billets; SANITARY SECTION lorry brought in for overhaul. Rained heavily in the evening.	ADSS
LES LOBES	25/10/15	6.0pm	Workshops running until 10 pm to complete repairs in hand; from bought in BETHUNE for lunch stretchers. Incessant rain.	ADSS
LES LOBES	26/10/15	6.0pm	A.D.M.S. asked to grant 7 days leave to ENGLAND to 6476 C.Q.M.Sgt. TAYLOR. 3 FIELD AMBULANCES asked to clothe M.T. Drivers in future; M.18538. M.S.S. PLATT received from 358 C. A.S.C. ST. OMER. Instructions received to transfer M.ZP338 Sgt. SEYMOUR S.W. to 358 C. A.S.C. ST. OMER; 100 gallons petrol from Railhead. Fine.	ADSS

WAR DIARY
or
INTELLIGENCE SUMMARY.
(Erase heading not required.)

Army Form C. 2118.

Place	Date	Hour	Summary of Events and Information	Remarks and references to Appendices
LES LOBES	27/10/15	6.0 p.m.	O.C. visited D.D. of S.T. and arranged for M/8538 M.S.S. PLATT. H. to be returned to 358 C. Q.S.C. ST. OMER and for M/2838 Sgt. SEYMOUR S.N. to be retained with this Unit. Men paid at 2 p.m. then given half holiday. Application for leave of absence for 6476 CQMSgt. TAYLOR D.G. temporarily refused by A.D.M.S. Raining all day.	1543
LES LOBES	28/10/15	6.0 p.m.	100 gallons of petrol from Railhead. M/14762 SUNBEAM car from DIVISIONAL TRAIN in for repair – sent out same day. Lorry from MEERUT DIVISIONAL SUPPLY COLUMN collided with O.C's car. Raining all day.	1543
LES LOBES	29/10/15	6.0 p.m.	Usual routine. Raining intermittently all day.	
LES LOBES	30/10/15	6.0 p.m.	150 galls of petrol from Railhead. Half holiday given to me. Raining.	1543
LES LOBES	31/10/15	6.0 p.m.	Church parade at 9.0 a.m. Usual routine. Several storms during the day.	1543

19ᵗʰ F.A.b.v.
vol: 2

121/7656

19ᵗʰ Division

Nov. 15

Nov. 1915

Army Form C. 2118.

WAR DIARY
or
INTELLIGENCE SUMMARY.
(Erase heading not required.)

Instructions regarding War Diaries and Intelligence Summaries are contained in F. S. Regs., Part II. and the Staff Manual respectively. Title pages will be prepared in manuscript.

Place	Date	Hour	Summary of Events and Information	Remarks and references to Appendices
LES LOBES	1/11/15	6.0.p.m.	Proposed to form a poker club amongst the N.C.O's and men; necessary tokens ordered. Usual Routine. Raining heavily all day.	
LES LOBES	2/11/15	6.0.p.m.	150 Gallons petrol from Railhead; War Diaries for July, August September and October 1915 despatched to D.A.G, G.H.Q. 3rd ECHELON by Registered post. Usual Routine. Raining heavily all day.	
LES LOBES	3/11/15	6.0.p.m.	Usual routine. Heavy rain.	
LES LOBES	4/11/15	6.0.p.m.	150 Gallons petrol from Railhead; 208 French Stretchers Traversee delivered to the D.A.D.O.S. as per instructions from the A.D.M.S. Usual routine. Dull - some rain.	
LES LOBES	5/11/15	6.0.p.m.	Rear cylinder for 2¾ H.P DOUGLAS motor cycle returned to ADVANCED M.T. DEPOT. Usual routine. Dull - some rain.	
LES LOBES	6/11/15	6.0.p.m.	Weekly returns compiled and despatched. Returns for D.D. of S.T. personally delivered by O.C. M2. 079843 Pte. CHARLTON W.G. awarded 7 days C.B. and extra duties for conduct to the prejudice of good order and military discipline - insolence to an N.C.O then attend Baths at LOCON. Fine.	

Instructions regarding War Diaries and Intelligence
Summaries are contained in F. S. Regs., Part II.
and the Staff Manual respectively. Title pages
will be prepared in manuscript.

WAR DIARY
or
INTELLIGENCE SUMMARY.
(Erase heading not required.)

Army Form C. 2118.

Place	Date	Hour	Summary of Events and Information	Remarks and references to Appendices
LES LOBES	7/11/15	6.0 p.m.	100 Gallons petrol from Railhead; Workshop engine overhauled; Usual routine; fine.	
LES LOBES	8/11/15	6.0 p.m.	Ambulance attached to the 57th FIELD AMBULANCE meets with slight accident with Ambulance attached to 12th MOTOR AMBULANCE CONVOY on BETHUNE. Reported to O.C. for action. Usual routine. Fine.	
LES LOBES	9/11/15	6.0 p.m.	150 Gallons petrol from Railhead; boots - shipskin lined received from D.A.D.O.S. for motor drivers; NORTH LANCS left billets and WARWICKS come in. Rained very heavily all the evening.	
LES LOBES	10/11/15	6.0 p.m.	Men paid at 2 p.m. Usual routine. Fine	
LES LOBES	11/11/15	6.0 p.m.	150 Gallons petrol from Railhead. Workshop running all night to overhaul "DAIMLER" lorry. Rained heavily all day.	
LES LOBES	12/11/15	6.0 p.m.	100 Gallons petrol from Railhead. Rained heavily all day.	
LES LOBES	13/11/15	6.0 p.m.	Weekly returns compiled and despatched; No. 057030. Pte. SHAW T.D. attends doctor. Usual routine. Fine but much colder.	
LES LOBES	14/11/15	6.0 p.m.	Men given half day's holiday; Usual Routine. Heavy frost.	

WAR DIARY or INTELLIGENCE SUMMARY.

Army Form C. 2118.

(Erase heading not required.)

Instructions regarding War Diaries and Intelligence Summaries are contained in F. S. Regs., Part II. and the Staff Manual respectively. Title pages will be prepared in manuscript.

Place	Date	Hour	Summary of Events and Information	Remarks and references to Appendices
LES LOBES	15/11/15	6.0 pm	Night shift working from 7-12 p.m. Fine frost.	1843
LES LOBES	16/11/15	6.0 pm	150 gallons of petrol from Railhead; meeting of the newly inaugurated "Paper Club" held in the evening, preceded over by the O.C. Usual routine. Some rain during the day.	1843
LES LOBES	17/11/15	6.0 pm	Men paid at 6.0 p.m. Draft suggestions for "Instructions to drivers" submitted by O.C. to D.A.Q.M.G., 19th DIVISION, in accordance with D of T. memo. No. 8459 dated 12/11/15. Usual routine. Heavy hoar storms during the day.	1843
LES LOBES	18/11/15	6.0 pm	"SINGER" car attached to the 19th DIVISIONAL SIGNALS towed to the Workshop for extensive repairs. Usual routine. Raining.	1843
LES LOBES	19/11/15	6.0 pm	100 gallons of petrol from Railhead. Unusual demand for tyres for Ambulances. Usual routine. Dull-cold.	1843
LES LOBES	20/11/15	6.0 pm	Returns compiled and despatched. Returns for D.D. of S.& T. personally delivered by O.C. Front spring of "DAIMLER" lorry broken. Fine bright.	1843
LES LOBES	21/11/15	6.0 pm	Usual routine. Dull, but no rain.	1843

WAR DIARY
or
INTELLIGENCE SUMMARY.
(Erase heading not required.)

Army Form C. 2118.

Place	Date	Hour	Summary of Events and Information	Remarks and references to Appendices
LES LOBES	22/11/15	6.0 p.m.	O.C., visited A.D.M.S. with regard to moving with the remainder of the division. Usual routine. Fine, bright. Fog in the evening.	
LES LOBES	23/11/15	6.0 p.m.	Men given half holiday. Weather changed. Rain in the evening.	
LES LOBES } MERVILLE }	24/11/15	6.0 p.m.	Packed up and left LES LOBES at 11 a.m. Arrived MERVILLE 12 o'clock. Vehicle parked in PLACE DE L'EGLISE. Men billeted in content. Rain and heavy hail storms.	
MERVILLE	25/11/15	6.0 p.m.	Stores unpacked and straightened up. Application for leave for 6476 - C.Q.M. Sgt. TAYLOR D.G., submitted to A.D.M.S. Instructions received by O.C., from D.H.Q. to carry out electric light installation at the CHATEAU, ST. VENANT. Heavy storms during the day.	
MERVILLE } ST. VENANT }	26/11/15	6.0 p.m.	Packed up and left MERVILLE at 12 o'clock. Arrived ST. VENANT. 1.0 p.m. encountering heavy hail and snow storm "en route". Vehicles parked by L'HOTEL DE VILLE. Men billeted at Estaminet. Freezing.	
ST. VENANT	27/11/15	6.0 p.m.	Stores unpacked and suitably arranged. Intimation received from A.D.M.S. that this UNIT will be attached to the 57th FIELD AMBULANCE on and after DEC 1st 1915. Warrant for C.Q.M.S. TAYLOR received. Freezing hard all day.	

WAR DIARY
or
INTELLIGENCE SUMMARY.

(Erase heading not required.)

Army Form C. 2118.

Instructions regarding War Diaries and Intelligence Summaries are contained in F.S. Regs., Part II. and the Staff Manual respectively. Title pages will be prepared in manuscript.

Place	Date	Hour	Summary of Events and Information	Remarks and references to Appendices
ST. VENANT	28/11/15	6.0 pm	Return of MOTOR AMBULANCES sent to A.D.M.S. Usual routine. Freezing hard all day.	S.A.B
ST. VENANT	29/11/15	6.0 pm	6476 - C.Q.M.S. TAYLOR. D.G. proceeded on leave of absence until DECEMBER 6th 1915. 150 Gallons of Petrol from Railhead. Electric lighting at CHATEAU completed, tested, and found to be satisfactory. Weather changed, rain and hail during the day.	S.A.B
ST. VENANT	30/11/15	6.0 pm	M 28338. SGT. SEYMOUR. S.N., M² 052030 - PTE. SHAW. R.D., M² 082077 PTE BUTLER G.T. Severely admonished by O.C. for drawing money from THE FIELD CASHIER at MERVILLE without O.C.'s knowledge when paid at 2 p.m. Usual routine. Dull.	S.A.B

19th Division

19th F.A. W.U.
Vol. 3

121/7911

1 Dec. 1915

Army Form C. 2118.

WAR DIARY
or
INTELLIGENCE SUMMARY.
(Erase heading not required.)

Instructions regarding War Diaries and Intelligence Summaries are contained in F. S. Regs., Part II. and the Staff Manual respectively. Title pages will be prepared in manuscript.

Place	Date	Hour	Summary of Events and Information	Remarks and references to Appendices
ST. VENANT	1/12/15	6.0 p.m.	FIELD AMBULANCES asked to send ACTIVE SERVICE LOG BOOKS to WORKSHOP every Monday morning to facilitate entries. Duplicate receipt for 119f 60c obtained from BOUQUET EVIN, BETHUNE at August of PAYMASTER, BASE. Draft forms for weekly repair and replacement returns submitted to A.D.M.S. for approval. Workshop running for electric light at CHATEAU. Usual routine. Dull rain.	NB
ST. VENANT	2/2/15	6.0 p.m.	6476. C.Q.M. Sgt. TAYLOR. D.G. informed of the altered time of boat train. M.28336 Lce. Corpl. (Acting Sergt). SEYMOUR. S.W. transferred to G.H.Q. TROOPS SUPPLY COLUMN in accordance with instructions received from DD. of S.T. 150 gallons of petrol from Railhead. Mild, raining all day.	NB
ST. VENANT	3/2/15	6.0 p.m.	Orders received from D.H.Q to proceed to LESTREM to erect and install electric light at CHATEAU. early on Sunday morning. Billeting certificate handed to the Mayor of ST. VENANT. Raining hard all day.	NB
ST. VENANT	4/2/15	6.0 p.m.	Returns compiled and despatched. SUNBEAM car attached to 57th FIELD AMBULANCE broken down on road at PARADIS. Stores partially packed in readiness to move. 150 gallons of petrol from Railhead. Raining all day.	NB

WAR DIARY
or
INTELLIGENCE SUMMARY.
(Erase heading not required.)

Army Form C. 2118.

Place	Date	Hour	Summary of Events and Information	Remarks and references to Appendices
ST. VENANT LOCON	5/2/15	6.0 p.m.	Packed up and left ST. VENANT at 11.0 a.m; arrived LOCON. 12 o'clock. Workshops and stores taken to TOBACCO FACTORY and men billeted there. Raining heavily from 5.0 p.m.	
LOCON	6/2/15	6.0 p.m.	Stores unpacked and straightened up. M².079845. Acting Corpl. STADDEN J.T. reports sick. Wires in connection with electric installation fixed at CHATEAU, LESTREM. 100 Gallons Petrol from Railhead. Raining intermittently all day.	
LOCON	7/2/15	6.0 p.m.	Acting Corpl. STADDEN J.T. again reports sick. Weekly returns of repairs and replacements to Motor Ambulances sent to the A.D.M.S. for the first time. 100 gallons of petrol from Railhead. Usual routine. Raining all day.	
LOCON	8/2/15	6.0 p.m.	M².079845. Acting Corpl. STADDEN J.T. to hospital. Then paid at 2.0 p.m. BUCKINGHAMSHIRE car brought in with broken body. Orders received through DD of S+T to transfer SUNBEAM car No. M.T.15094 to 46ᴬ Divn Ammn Sub Park in exchange for DAIMLER CAR No. M.T.5571. DOUGLAS motor cycle frame No. 24817 received from 19ᵗʰ Divl. Supply Column. Fine.	

Army Form C. 2118.

WAR DIARY
or
INTELLIGENCE SUMMARY.
(Erase heading not required.)

Instructions regarding War Diaries and Intelligence Summaries are contained in F. S. Regs., Part II. and the Staff Manual respectively. Title pages will be prepared in manuscript.

Place	Date	Hour	Summary of Events and Information	Remarks and references to Appendices
LOCON	9/7/15	6.0 p.m.	150 Gallons of petrol from Railhead. DOUGLAS motor cycle frame No. 20983 returned to SUPPLY COLUMN and cycle No. 24817 sent to 58th FIELD AMBULANCE. Exchange of SUNBEAM for DAIMLER not effected, on account of the latter having a broken strut cycle. On return of 6476. C.Q.M. Sgt. TAYLOR. D.G. reported to A.D.M.S. Rain during the evening and gale all day.	
LOCON	10/7/15	6.0 p.m.	Mr 0820qq Pte BUTLER G.T. evacuated sick from 59th FIELD AMBULANCE. Nr 081442 Pte SADLER S. to hospital. 6476- C.Q.M. Sgt- TAYLOR D.G. still absent. Orders received through D.D. of S.+T. to exchange SUNBEAM motor Ambulance for NAPIER Ambulance attached to the 46th DIVL AMBULANCE WORKSHOP. Several heavy storms during the day.	
LOCON LESTREM	11/7/15	6.0 p.m.	Mr 079915 Pte BROWN J.S. to be ACTING LANCE-CORPORAL; Packed up and left TOBACCO FACTORY at 11.36 a.m.; arrived LESTREM at 12.15 p.m.; Workshops and Stores parked outside CHATEAU. Electric light satisfactorily supplied to the CHATEAU; Letter received from 6476 C.Q.M. Sgt TAYLOR. D.G. stating he was in MILITARY HOSPITAL, SHORNCLIFFE, about to undergo an operation. A.D.M.S. duly informed. Duel	

WAR DIARY
or
INTELLIGENCE SUMMARY.
(Erase heading not required.)

Army Form C. 2118.

Place	Date	Hour	Summary of Events and Information	Remarks and references to Appendices
LESTREM	12/2/15	6.0 pm	Stores unpacked and straightened up. Instructions received from D.H.Q. to wire up theatre for 19th DIVISIONAL "FOLLIES", by tomorrow night. From spring of DAIMLER lorry broken. Guard re-arranged on a more satisfactory basis. Weather changed, much colder.	for B
LESTREM	13/2/15	6.0 pm	DOUGLAS motor cycle, Frame No. 17937 sent to SUPPLY COLUMN for exchange. m: 081442 Pte SADLER. S returned from hospital. O.C. called out to breakdown of SUNBEAM on road between ARQUES and AIRE. at 10.p.m. SGT. CRAWFORD. A.T. away from duty all day on account of illness. Hand foot.	for B
LESTREM	14/2/15	6.0 pm	O.C. and fitters returned from there at 11.30 am after unsuccessful hunt for breakdown. DAIMLER Car MT 9571 broke down on road, which delayed. O.C. for 5½ hours. Further search made in the afternoon, but no car found. Returned to Workshops at 10.0 pm. Return of repairs and replacements to Motor Ambulances sent to A.D.M.S. Very cold, but fine.	for B
LESTREM	15/2/15	6.0 pm	Intimation received from O.C. 59th FIELD AMBULANCE that SUNBEAM ambulance C.16. had returned to Unit, having been repaired by a Mobile Workshop on the road. Usual routine. Dull and cold.	for B

WAR DIARY
or
INTELLIGENCE SUMMARY.
(Erase heading not required.)

Army Form C. 2118.

Place	Date	Hour	Summary of Events and Information	Remarks and references to Appendices
LESTREM	16/2/15	6.0pm	A.D.M.S. informed of the unsatisfactory condition of the Ambulance Cars attached to the 59th FIELD AMBULANCE. Then paid at 5pm. Fine but cold.	A.B
LESTREM	17/2/15	6.0pm	M² 080723. Act. Corpl. SMAILUM. R.T. to be ACTING SERGT. T11915 DAIMLER lorry sent to TYRE PRESS ISBERGUES to be re-tyred. M² 079915. Act. Lce. Cpl. BROWN. J.S. admonished by C.O. for driving DAIMLER lorry without a "Loof-out" man. Case reported by A.P.M. 19th DIV 18/10/1. Officer's Car laid up. Usual routine. Frost broken, quite mild.	A.B
LESTREM	18/2/15	6.0pm	Weekly returns completed. O.C. visited D.D. of S.+T taking with him weekly returns and two SUNBEAM springs. 34380. Pte WALBUTTON. C. and 35380. Pte. FEADE. H. received from O.C. 58th FIELD AMBULANCE for test as motor drivers. DAIMLER lorry T11915 returned from ISBERGUES at 6pm. "NAPIER" Ambulance brought to Workshop with broken back spring. Arrangements made with A.D.M.S. to call in One Ambulance daily for inspection. Dull - mild.	A.B
LESTREM	19/2/15	6.0pm	Two men received from 58th FIELD AMBULANCE tested on DAIMLER lorry and found to be satisfactory. Usual routine. Fine but cold.	A.B

WAR DIARY
or
INTELLIGENCE SUMMARY.
(Erase heading not required.)

Army Form C. 2118.

Place	Date	Hour	Summary of Events and Information	Remarks and references to Appendices
LESREM	20/2/15	6.0pm	Lindur bought for Sunbeam Ambulance presented by the LADIES OF BUCKINGHAM-SHIRE and two Ford Cars. N° 081442 Pte SADLER S. complained of bad Language used by N° 079396 Pte. LOCKE N.C. Reprimanded by O.C. and placed in a lower position on the leave roll. Dull but cold.	two
LESTREM	21/2/15	5.0pm	Weekly return of repairs and replacements to Motor Ambulances sent to the A.D.M.S. First Motor Ambulance called in for inspection in accordance with the arrangement made with the A.D.M.S. O.C. submits application to A.D.M.S. for promotion. Usual routine. Raining intermittently all day but mild.	two
LESTREM	22/2/15	5.0pm	Notification received that FODEN Steam Lorry attached to the 19th DIVL. SANITARY SECTION is to be supplied with oil spares etc. then paid at 2.pm. FORD new parts received from M.T.DEPOT, CALAIS. Drizzling all day but quite mild.	two
LESTREM	23/2/15	6.0pm	DAIMLER Lorry T5922 attached to 19th DIVISIONAL SANITARY SECTION sent to TYRE PRESS, ISBERGUES to be re-tyred. Cheque value £7-14-6 sent to PAYMASTER, I/c CLEARING HOUSE, BASE, in settlement of balance of outstanding a/c. Raining all day. Usual routine.	two

WAR DIARY
or
INTELLIGENCE SUMMARY.
(Erase heading not required.)

Army Form C. 2118.

Place	Date	Hour	Summary of Events and Information	Remarks and references to Appendices
LESTREM	25/7/15	6.0pm	Cash + Pay. Issue Books returned to PAYMASTER BASE by Registered Post. Men worked late to clear up work at the Workshops. Some rain during the day. Mild	W.D.
LESTREM	26/7/15	6.0pm	Men commenced work at 9.0. am and finished at 3.30.p.m. Returns compiled and despatched. O.D. of S.T. returns sent by D.R.L.S. to rain - mild	W.D.
LESTREM	26/7/15	6.0pm	Officer's Car in the Workshop for overhaul. Indents compiled and despatched. Usual routine. Dull. Some rain.	W.D.
LESTREM	27/7/15	6.0pm	No. 052030 Pte. SHAW R.D. taken ill at Workshops and taken to Hospital. Usual routine. Dull. No rain.	W.D.
LESTREM	28/7/15	6.0pm	No. 052030 Pte. SHAW. R.D. evacuated by 59th FIELD AMBULANCE. DOUGLAS motor cycles, Frame Nos. 22565 + 19539 sent to 19th DIV. SUPPLY COLUMN. for replacement. Morning parade at 7.30 ordered. Weekly return of repairs and replacements to Motor Ambulance sent to A.D.M.S. DOUGLAS motor cycle received from SUPPLY COLUMN and forwarded to 59th FIELD AMBULANCE. Fine, but windy.	W.D.

WAR DIARY
or
INTELLIGENCE SUMMARY.
(Erase heading not required.)

Army Form C. 2118.

Place	Date	Hour	Summary of Events and Information	Remarks and references to Appendices
LESTREM	29/7/15	6.0 pm	Sgt. NASH T. no. 079913 sentenced to 14 days C.B. and extra duties for dis- -obedience to orders and conduct to the prejudice of good order and military discipline 8/8/5/9. Pte MILNE N (letter); 9/11030. Pte PATERSON G. (fitter) 8929. Pte GARTSIDE J (driver) and M² 151651, Pte SNELLING A.E. (driver) received from BASE. M.T. DEPÔT. ROUEN. Usual routine, some rain.	
LESTREM	30/7/15	6.0 pm	Full report of circumstances surrounding the absence of 6476 - C.Q.M.S₁- TAYLOR.D.B. sent to Colonel, I/c A.S.C. SECTION, A.G's Office at the BASE. Work slackens down at Workshops. Dull but fine.	
LESTREM	31/7/15	6.0 pm	Monthly returns compiled; usual routine; Raining during the evening.	

19th F.A.W.U.
Vol. 4

Jan 1916

WAR DIARY
or
INTELLIGENCE SUMMARY.

(Erase heading not required.)

Army Form C. 2118.

Place	Date	Hour	Summary of Events and Information	Remarks and references to Appendices
LESTREM	1/1/16	6.0 pm	Monthly and weekly Returns compiled and despatched; O.C. delivers weekly return to D.D. of S.T. War Diary for December despatched. New March Card Paro No. 9782 received from A.P.M. Old paros No. 11186 duly destroyed. Some rain during the day.	SR
LESTREM	2/1/16	6.0 pm	Indents Compiled and despatched. M.T. OP 2077, Pte. BUTLER G.T. returned from hospital DAIMLER Car No MT 9571 exchanged for SUNBEAM car No MT 15790 on authority of D.D.S.T. Raining all day with heavy gales.	SR
LESTREM	3/1/16	6.0 pm	A.F. B122 received from MT DEPOT ROUEN in respect of three lorries. Usual routine. Dull mild.	SR
LESTREM	4/1/16	6.0 pm	Electrical fittings fixed at LA GORGUE for performance of "19th DIVL. FOLLIES". Usual routine. fine.	SR
LESTREM	5/1/16	6.0 pm	Lt. BRADLEY proceeded on leave of absence to ENGLAND. Lt. GRANT-DALTON of 19th DIVL SUPPLY COLUMN visited Workshop in afternoon to supervise. Electrical fittings fetched from LA GORGUE and fixed at LESTREM. Some rain during the day.	SR

WAR DIARY
or
INTELLIGENCE SUMMARY.

(Erase heading not required.)

Army Form C. 2118.

Place	Date	Hour	Summary of Events and Information	Remarks and references to Appendices
LESTREM	6/1/16	6.0pm	New stirrups for BUCKINGHAMSHIRE car fetched from STEENBECQUE. Usual routine. Dull, but no rain.	BM
LESTREM	7/1/16	6.0pm	No. 050442. Pte. STANLEY A.T. brought to orderly room for absence from morning parade and disobedience to standing orders. Was paid at 8 pm. Dull rain during the day.	BM
LESTREM	8/1/16	6.0pm	Weekly returns completed and despatched. Returns for D.D.S.T. taken by Lt. GRANT DALTON. No. 082077. Pte. BUTLER. G.T. to Hospital. Usual routine. Dull.	BM
LESTREM	9/1/16	6.0pm	Indent completed and despatched. Usual routine. Rained during the morning.	BM
LESTREM	10/1/16	6.0pm	Usual routine. Fine and mild.	BM
LESTREM	11/1/16	6.0pm	No. 081445 Pte. SADLER. S. reports sick. No. 082077 Pte. BUTLER G.T. returned from Hospital. Weekly return of repair and replacements to Motor Ambulances sent to A.D.M.S. Storm in the afternoon.	BM
LESTREM	12/1/16	6.0pm	Lt. BRADLEY returned from leave of absence at 8.30 pm. Usual routine. Rained during the evening.	BM

WAR DIARY
or
INTELLIGENCE SUMMARY.

(Erase heading not required.)

Army Form C. 2118.

Place	Date	Hour	Summary of Events and Information	Remarks and references to Appendices
LESTREM	13/1/16	6.0pm	A.F.B.122 in respect of PTE SNELLING received from M.T.DEPOT. ROUEN. Officers Car overhauled. Usual routine. Weather unsettled but mild.	154
LESTREM	14/1/16	6.0pm	M².078110. Acting SERGT. CRAWFORD A.T. to be ACTING STAFF SERGT. with SERGT's Pay. Men paid at 2 pm. Usual routine. Some rain during the evening.	154
LESTREM	15/1/16	6.0pm	M².050442 PTE. STANLEY A.T. Sentenced to 21 days No. 2 FIELD PUNISHMENT by O.C. 57th FIELD AMBULANCE for disobedience to orders and insolence to an N.C.O. Weekly returns completed and despatched. Returns for D.D.S.T. sent by D.R.L.S. then given half holiday. Fine and mild.	154 154
LESTREM	16/1/16	6.0pm	M².080723 SERGT. SNAILUM. R.T. proceeded on leave of absence. Fine.	154
LESTREM	17/1/16	6.0pm	O.C's Car broke down on road – new spring fitted. Return called for by A.D.M.S. Re non-delivery of goods by M.T.DEPOT. Wet.	152 154
LESTREM	18/1/16	6.0pm	Usual routine. Wet.	
LESTREM	19/1/16	6.0pm	Entered sidings from STEENBECQUE. Arranged billets at ROBECQUE. Fine. Cold wind.	154

WAR DIARY
or
INTELLIGENCE SUMMARY.
(Erase heading not required.)

Army Form C. 2118.

Place	Date	Hour	Summary of Events and Information	Remarks and references to Appendices
LESTREM	20/1/16	6.0 p.m.	New billets inspected and sanctioned by A.D.M.S. Usual routine. Fine.	[1A] [1B]
LESTREM	21/1/16	6.0 p.m.	Usual routine. Fine.	[1B]
LESTREM	22/1/16	6.0 p.m.	Weekly return compiled and despatched. Strings fetched from STEENBECQUE then given half holiday. Fine.	[1B] [1B]
LESTREM	23/1/16	6.0 p.m.	Picked up ready to move to ROBECQUE.	[1B]
LESTREM	24/1/16	6.0 p.m.	Moved to ROBECQUE. Vehicles parked in farms and men billeted. Fine but colder.	[1B]
ROBECQUE LESTREM	25/1/16	6.0 p.m.	N°. 080723 - SGT. SNAILUM. R.T. returned from leave of absence having been granted an extra days leave on account of delay at BOULOGNE. Fine.	[1B]
ROBECQUE LESTREM	26/1/16	6.0 p.m.	Nominal roll of Unit called for from A.G.'s OFFICE at the BASE. Usual routine. Fine.	[12A]
ROBECQUE LESTREM	27/1/16	6.0 p.m.	Men paid at 2.30 p.m. Billeting certificate despatched. Usual routine. Fine.	[1B]
ROBECQUE	28/1/16	6.0 p.m.	Front spring of DAIMLER lorry broken. Usual routine. Fine.	[1B]

WAR DIARY
or
INTELLIGENCE SUMMARY.
(Erase heading not required.)

Army Form C. 2118.

Place	Date	Hour	Summary of Events and Information	Remarks and references to Appendices
ROBECQUE	29/1/16	6.0 p.m.	Weekly returns completed and despatched. O.C. personally delivered returns to D.D. of S. & T. Spring for Daimler lorry obtained from STEENBECQUE. Staff Sergt CRAWFORD and Cpl MARLOW (culleries) for slackness. Usual routine. Fine.	
ROBECQUE	30/1/16	6.0 p.m.	M². 080276. Pte LOWE. J reports sick and is retained in Hospital. M². 052.965. Pte JONES R.M reports sick but is not retained. M². 052030. Pte SHAW R.D. arrives from ROUEN, but immediately reports sick, and is at once evacuated by the 57th FIELD AMBULANCE. Usual routine. Cold and misty.	
ROBECQUE	31/1/16	6.0 p.m.	Monthly returns completed. Usual routine. Fine and cold.	

19th Y.A.W.U.

Feb 1916

19th F.a.w.v.
Vol 5

WAR DIARY
or
INTELLIGENCE SUMMARY.
(Erase heading not required.)

Army-Form C. 2118.

Instructions regarding War Diaries and Intelligence Summaries are contained in F.S. Regs., Part II. and the Staff Manual respectively. Title pages will be prepared in manuscript.

Place	Date	Hour	Summary of Events and Information	Remarks and references to Appendices
ROBECQUE	1.2.16	6.0 pm	Monthly returns compiled & despatched. M⁰ 080076 Pte. LOVE. J. returned from Hospital. Then finished work at 4.0 pm. Usual Routine. Fine but very cold.	SNB
ROBECQUE	2.2.16	6.0 pm	Usual Routine. Fine.	SNB
ROBECQUE	3.2.16	6.0 pm	Men given half Holiday. Fine.	SNB
ROBECQUE	4.2.16	6.0 pm	M⁰ 079915. ACTING LCE-CPL BROWN. J.S. to be ACTING CPL without pay. M⁰ 079607 ACTING CPL MARLOW. J. reduced to permanent grade for disobedience to orders. M⁰ 053030 Pte. SHAW. F.D. returned from Hospital. Men paid at 9.30 a.m. Usual routine. Rained heavily during the evening.	
ROBECQUE	5.2.16	6.0 pm	Weekly returns compiled and despatched. O.C. personally delivered returns to DD of S.& T. Pte. SHAW. F.D. Cautioned for slackness in Saluting. Wet.	SNB
ROBECQUE	6.2.16	6.0 pm	M⁰ 079110. Actg M.S.S. CRANFORD. A.R. proceeded on leave of absence to England. Men worked until 6.0 p.m. Wet. Ending compiled & despatched. Drizzling all day.	SNB
ROBECQUE	7.2.16	6.0 pm	Workshops running till 8.0 pm. Lorry sent out at 5.0 pm. to bring in broken down motor-cycle attached to the 59th F.A. Rained hard all day.	SNB

Army Form C. 2118.

WAR DIARY
or
INTELLIGENCE SUMMARY.
(Erase heading not required.)

Instructions regarding War Diaries and Intelligence Summaries are contained in F. S. Regs., Part II. and the Staff Manual respectively. Title pages will be prepared in manuscript.

Place	Date	Hour	Summary of Events and Information	Remarks and references to Appendices
ROBECQUE	8.2.16	6.0 p.m.	Dmr.² 130334. Pte. DRAKE. N.T. (Arnie) received from ROUEN. O.C., visited D.A.Q.M.G. and arranged for lighting at LA GORGUE. Workshops running until 4.0 p.m. Rained hard all day and froze at night.	W.B
ROBECQUE	9.2.16	6.0 p.m.	Workshops running until 5.0 p.m. Lighting set received from SIGNALS. Weather unsettled - cold.	W.B
ROBECQUE	10.2.16	6.0 p.m.	Both front springs of DAIMLER lorry broken. O.C. Car in for overhaul. D.D. of S.+T. called for nurses return of "PARTS, URGENTLY REQUIRED." Occasional storms during the day.	W.B
ROBECQUE	11.2.16	6.0 p.m.	Springs for DAIMLER lorry obtained from STEENBECQUE. Usual routine. Rained heavily all day.	W.B
ROBECQUE	12.2.16	6.0 p.m.	M².080276 - Pte. LOWE J. to Hospital. Nearly returns completed. O.C., delivered returns to D.D. of S.+T., and obtained authority to transfer NAPIER AMBULANCE No. A.1950S, attached to the 5th F.A. Nominal roll of artificers sent to A.G.'s OFFICE. BASE. Fine, but colder.	W.B
ROBECQUE	13.2.16	6.0 p.m.	Dvr.² 130344. Pte. DRAKE N.T. transferred to 19th DIVL. SUPPLY COLUMN. Men finished roof at H.Q. pm. Fine.	W.B

T2134. Wt. W708—776. 500000. 4/15. Sir J. C. & S.

WAR DIARY
or
INTELLIGENCE SUMMARY.
(Erase heading not required.)

Army-Form C. 2118.

Instructions regarding War Diaries and Intelligence Summaries are contained in F. S. Regs., Part II. and the Staff Manual respectively. Title pages will be prepared in manuscript.

Place	Date	Hour	Summary of Events and Information	Remarks and references to Appendices
ROBECQUE	14.2.16	6.0pm	M².057969. Pte. SIMS. N.G. to hospital. M².078110 Act.M.S.S. CRANFORD A.R. returns from leave of absence. A.D.M.S. calls for report re NAPIER Ambulance. Usual routine. Fine and windy.	A.R
ROBECQUE	15.2.16	6.0pm	Men finished work at 4.0 pm. Rained hard in the morning and evening. Heavy gales.	A.R
ROBECQUE	16.2.16	6.0pm	Packed up ready to move at 9 o'clock to-morrow morning. Some rain during the day.	A.R
MERVILLE	17.2.16	6.0pm	Left ROBECQUE at 9.0 am. Arrived MERVILLE at 12 o'clock. Trouble with PEERLESS lorries en route. Notebooks packed at position on MAP SHEET 36A – 3rd EDITION – K29A.7.7. Weather fine but very cold.	B.C
MERVILLE	18.2.16	6.0pm	Stores unpacked and straightened up. Rained hard all day.	B.C
MERVILLE	19.2.16	6.0pm	North returns compiled & despatched. Usual routine. Dull but no rain.	A.R
MERVILLE	20.2.16	6.0pm	M².080276. Pte LOWE J. evacuated from ST⁴.F.A. to No 3½ CASUALTY CLEARING STATION. M².057969. Pte. SIMS. N.G. returned from hospital. Usual routine. Rained heavily during the day.	A.R

WAR DIARY
or
INTELLIGENCE SUMMARY

Army Form C. 2118.

Place	Date	Hour	Summary of Events and Information	Remarks and references to Appendices
MERVILLE	21.2.16	6.0 pm	Gas lighting arranged for Recreation Room at LA GORQUE. Napier Ambulance No. A 9505 evacuated to PARIS with two drivers. D.D. of S+T asked to replace with SUNBEAM ambulance, if possible. Usual routine. Dull but calm.	ADMS
MERVILLE	22.2.16	6.0 pm	Heavy Snow-Storm during the morning and afternoon. Lighting arrangement at LA GORQUE completed. Usual routine.	ADMS
MERVILLE	23.2.16	6.0 pm	Snow storm during the morning. Usual routine	ADMS
MERVILLE	24.2.16	6.0 pm	Froze hard all day. Men crowded re Lorries of Guard during meal times. Usual routine.	ADMS
MERVILLE	25.2.16	6.0 pm	Return of Cars fit for the road sent to A.D.M.S. Heavy snow storm during the evening. Usual routine.	ADMS
MERVILLE	26.2.16	6.0 pm	Returns completed. O.C. personally delivered returns to D.D. of S+T. Usual routine. Snow.	ADMS
MERVILLE	27.2.16	6.0 pm	O.C. visited STEENBECQUE re springs for DAIMLER lorry. Usual routine. Mild.	ADMS
MERVILLE	28.2.16	6.0 pm	Return sent to A.D.M.S. Usual routine. Some rain during the evening.	ADMS
MERVILLE	29.2.16	6.0 pm	Monthly returns completed. Usual routine. Mild - rained slightly during afternoon + evening.	ADMS

WAR DIARIES

of

19th Divisional Field Ambulance Workshop Unit - A.S.C.,

for the

Months of March and April 1916

19th Div
F A 3
V 6 D

COMMITTEE FOR THE
MEDICAL HISTORY OF THE WAR
Date 9-JUN.'915

Per Registered Post

To: D.A.G.,
    G.H.Q.,
    3rd Echelon.

I herewith beg to forward A.F's. C2118 in respect of the Unit under my Command, for the month of March 1916.

Munro 2nd Lt.
         A.S.C. M.T.
O.C. 19th Divl. Ambulance Workshops

19 D W F A W O Army Form C. 2118.

WAR DIARY
or
INTELLIGENCE SUMMARY.
(Erase heading not required.)

Instructions regarding War Diaries and Intelligence Summaries are contained in F. S. Regs., Part II. and the Staff Manual respectively. Title pages will be prepared in manuscript.

Place	Date	Hour	Summary of Events and Information	Remarks and references to Appendices
MERVILLE	1/3/16	6.0pm	Consumption of 10,000 gallons of petrol reached since disembarkation, showing an approximate mileage of 100,000 miles. Monthly returns despatched. O.C. fetched sponge for DAIMLEY lorry from STEENBECQUE. New Car Pass No 9311 received by O.C. from A.P.M. Usual routine. Fine.	
MERVILLE	2/3/16	6.0pm.	Circular received from D.D. of S.T. requesting weekly return of petrol consumption of all vehicles attached to the Unit. O.C. interviewed A.D.M.S. with a view to obtaining the necessary information from O.C.s FIELD AMBULANCES. Usual routine. Fine.	
MERVILLE	3/3/16	6.0pm.	Mr. 079915 - Acting Corpl. BROWN. J.S. admonished by O.C. for leaving DAIMLEY lorry in streets of MERVILLE unattended. Reported by A.P.M., 11th Corps. Motorcycles running until 8pm; Very heavy storm during the afternoon and evening.	
MERVILLE	4/3/16	6.0pm	Weekly returns completed. O.C. delivered returns to D.D of S.T. Napier Ambulance W.D. No. A.7956 received from D.D. of S.T., to replace Napier Ambulance recently evacuated to PARIS. Car duly delivered to 57th FIELD AMBULANCE together with M1/5731 - Pte MOSS. N. Motorcycles running until 7pm. Heavy snow storm during the morning.	

WAR DIARY
or
INTELLIGENCE SUMMARY.
(Erase heading not required.)

Army Form C. 2118.

Place	Date	Hour	Summary of Events and Information	Remarks and references to Appendices
MERVILLE	5/3/16	6.0pm	Trains despatched. Usual Routine. Rained and snowed slightly during the afternoon.	Apx W
MERVILLE	6/3/16	6.0pm	M/0199946 - Pte ASHWORTH. J.H. received from 19th Divl. SUPPLY COLUMN and posted to 19th Divl. SANITARY SECTION to replace casualty. Usual routine. Heavy snow storms during the day.	Apx W
MERVILLE	7/3/16	6.0pm	M/086576 Pte LOW. E. J, received as re-inforcement from M.T. DEPOT, ROUEN, thus bringing Unit up to full strength. Snowed all day without cessation.	Apx W
MERVILLE	8/3/16	6.0pm	M/082919 Pte BURTON. P. received from 19th Divl. SUPPLY COLUMN and posted to 57th FIELD AMBULANCE. A.F.o.B.122. in respect of 6476 - C.Q.M.S. TAYLOR. D.T.; M/079845 - Acting Corpl. STADDON. J.T.; M/081445 - Pte SADLER. S. posted to A.G's OFFICE AT THE BASE. Fine, frost hard at night. Usual routine.	Apx W
MERVILLE	9/3/16	6.0pm	M/076701 - Pte ELLERY. L. received from No 4 & 57th FIELD AMBULANCE and transferred to 19th Divl. SUPPLY COLUMN. 2nd Lt. M.E. BRADLEY admitted to hospital. Lt. GRANT-DALTON takes over management of Unit. Usual routine. Dull but no rain.	Apx W

WAR DIARY
or
INTELLIGENCE SUMMARY.
(Erase heading not required.)

Army Form C. 2118.

Place	Date	Hour	Summary of Events and Information	Remarks and references to Appendices
MERVILLE	10/3/16	6.0pm.	DAIMLER lorry attached to 19th DIVL. SANITARY SECTION received for re-tyring. Sent to ISBERGUES. 2nd Lt. M.E.BRADLEY evacuated from 16 Base Hospital. Usual routine - Dull but no rain.	clw
MERVILLE	11/3/16	6.0pm.	Weekly returns compiled. O.C., 19th DIVL. SUPPLY COLUMN delivered returns to D.D. of S.T. Return of mileage and petrol consumption of Motor Ambulances rendered for the first time. Usual routine. Dull.	clw
MERVILLE	12/3/16	6.0pm	Trains compiled and despatched. Fine. warm.	clw
MERVILLE	13/3/16	6.0pm	NAPIER Ambulance No. A T9596 broke down on road - broken spring. A.F.B.122 of THE MOSS issued and passed on to 57th FIELD AMBULANCE. Bright.	clw
MERVILLE	14/3/16	6.0pm.	SUNBEAM Ambulance attached to 59th FIELD AMBULANCE broke down on road - broken spring. Bright.	clw
MERVILLE	15/3/16	6.0pm	Men paid at 2 pm. Usual routine. Fine.	clw
MERVILLE	16/3/16	6.0pm	Motorcycles very busy. Warm but dull.	clw
MERVILLE	17/3/16	6.0pm	Return of Lorries (M.T) sent to D.D. of S.T. Usual routine. Fine. Bright.	clw

WAR DIARY
or
INTELLIGENCE SUMMARY.
(Erase heading not required.)

Army Form C. 2118.

Instructions regarding War Diaries and Intelligence Summaries are contained in F. S. Regs., Part II. and the Staff Manual respectively. Title pages will be prepared in manuscript.

Place	Date	Hour	Summary of Events and Information	Remarks and references to Appendices
MERVILLE	19/3/16	6.0pm	Returns compiled and despatched. O.C., SUPPLY COLUMN delivered returns to D.D. of S.+T. Usual routine. Rained during the evening.	—
MERVILLE	19/3/16	6.0pm	Events compiled and despatched. Workshops running until 8 p.m. Fine.	—
MERVILLE	20/3/16	6.0pm	Regimental number of S/8519 Pte. MILNE. W. altered to M²/162179 — Authority C.R/92454/DM dated 14/3/16. Arrangements made with A.D.M.S. re the repairing of Ambulance Cars. Ford Ambulance Car. No. C.20 broke down on the LA BASSÉE ROAD. — broken rear axle. Car towed to Workshops. Fine. Sunshine.	—
MERVILLE	21/3/16	6.0pm	Usual routine. Dull, but no rain.	—
MERVILLE	22/3/16	6.0pm	Men attended baths at 2 p.m. Usual routine. Raining all day.	—
MERVILLE	23/3/16	6.0pm	Instructors received from COLONEL, I/C. A.S.C. SECTION, BASE, to shew 6+76 — C.Q.M.S. TAYLOR as off the strength of the Unit. Usual routine. Fine. Allotment of M²/080733 — Act. Sgt SNAILUM. F.T. raised from 4- 5 4/6 per day from 19/1/16 " M²/078153 — Act. LCE COL. HANDSCOMBE. W.J.P. . 3/6 . 4/6 . " . 23/3/16 " M²/030111 — Pte STANLEY. A.T " " 4/- . 4/6 . " . 23/3/16	—

WAR DIARY
or
INTELLIGENCE SUMMARY.

Army Form C. 2118.

Place	Date	Hour	Summary of Events and Information	Remarks and references to Appendices
MERVILLE	24/3/16	6.0 pm	No. 052969. Pte. SIMS. N.G. to be ACTING LCE. CPL. without pay. Regimental number of S/11030. Pte PATERSON. G. altered to No. 162204. Authority CR./97183/D.N. dad 8/2/16. Snowed heavily throughout the morning. Usual routine.	em
MERVILLE	25/3/16	6.0 pm	Weekly returns compiled & despatched. Monthly return of cars fit for the road sent to A.D.M.S. Usual routine. Raining intermittently all day.	em
MERVILLE	26/3/16	6.0 pm	No. 079915- Act. CPL. BROWN J.S. proceeded on leave of absence till 3/4/16. Daimler lorry attached to 19th DIVL. SANITARY SECTION broken down at LA. GORQUE. - broken front spring. Men given half holiday. Unnecked.	em
MERVILLE	27/3/16	6.0 pm	2o.LT. C.MARTIN assumed Command of their Usual routine. Rained hard during the afternoon and evening.	em
MERVILLE	29/3/16	6.0 pm	O.C. visited FIELD AMBULANCES and inspected vehicles. Usual routine. Windy.	em
MERVILLE	29/3/16	6.0 pm	Men paid at 5 pm. Nonkehobo very busy. Fine but colder.	em
MERVILLE	30/3/16	6.0 pm	No. 162204 Pte. PATERSON G. and No. 162179 Pte. MILNE. N. admonished for "Conduct to the prejudice of good order and military discipline". O.C. visited STEENBECQUE re SUNBEAM springs. Fine - warmer.	em
MERVILLE	31/3/16	6.0 pm	Alterations to gas installation carried out at Recreation Room at LA.GORQUE. Usual routine. Fine.	em

19th Jan v
Vol 6
appendix

WAR DIARY
or
INTELLIGENCE SUMMARY.

(Erase heading not required.)

Army Form C. 2118.

Place	Date	Hour	Summary of Events and Information	Remarks and references to Appendices
MERVILLE	1/4/16	6.0pm	Weekly & monthly returns completed & despatched. O.C. delivered returns to D.D. of S&T. DOUGLAS motor cycle No. 80995 attached to 59th FIELD AMBULANCE evacuated to 19th DIVL SUPPLY COLUMN. Usual routine. Fine	98.
MERVILLE	2/4/16	6.0pm	DAIMLER lorry attached to SANITARY SECTION broken down on road at LA GORGUE - broken front spring. Men given half holiday. Fine.	98
MERVILLE	3/4/16	6.0pm	DOUGLAS motor cycle received in place of one evacuated on the 1st. Posted to 59th F.A. Usual routine. Fine	98
MERVILLE	4/4/16	6.0pm	2nd Lt. C. MARTIN proceeded on leave of absence M² 079915- ACTING CORPL. BROWN J.S. returned from leave of absence having been granted two extra days leave at BOULOGNE. Stores packed up & moved to 19th DIVL SUPPLY COLUMN Emperor ½ rotted up the bur colour. M² 079842 PTE CHARLTON N.G reports sick Wagons (Store - Workshop)	98
MERVILLE	5/4/16	6.0am	moved to SUPPLY COLUMN yard	98
MERVILLE	6/4/16	6.0am	Stores, Vehicles etc officially handed over to SUPPLY COLUMN. A.F.'s B122 also handed over	98

www.ingramcontent.com/pod-product-compliance
Lightning Source LLC
Chambersburg PA
CBHW081451160426
43193CB00013B/2440